the Rules
of
Blind
Obedience

Amirah Al Wassif

the Rules of Blind Obedience

GusGus Press • Bedazzled Ink Publishing
Fairfield, California

978-1-960373-56-4 paperback

Illustrations
by
Sarah Hussein

Cover Design
by

Sapling
Studio

GusGus Press
a division of
Bedazzled Ink Publishing Company
Fairfield, California
http://www.bedazzledink.com

Human tragedy

the holes that carved upon my forehead;
Reveal how old am I
My children had eaten their self
From a very young age.
I'm the mother
Who peels the hours
With the patience's knife.
Watching their severed heads
Sparkling from upstairs
Like stars.
I am the mother, I shout
Trying to call them by the name
My children are so many
Some on the trees
Some behind the clouds
Some riding horses in the sky
Some washing their bodies
In my veins.
Some rubbing their noses
In the heart of your fresh towels.
Although, they have died
For long centuries
There are no signs of
Their death.
No gravestones for them
I'm the only one
Who grieves over them
I'm here standing in pride
Don't come for finding me.
I'm the mother, I shout
The darkness cutting my throat.

I'm the detailed tale
My children aren't your bruises
They are the rhythm of
Your breath
Although, they all died
This isn't the end of the world.
We must have fun
Sometimes you have to turn
Your lights off
For the sake of
Bathing in the moonlight

Diaries from jail

Between my teeth, there is a gap
That kind could disturb a whole content.
My history began the very moment I escaped away from the herd.
When the leaves of our trees turned from green to red.
When our leader's head became our new sun.
The children circled around me, pushing me violently with such a great force.
They have believed the rumors which said I belong to the dangerous genre who dares to dream.
I have been trapped by the religious gang.
I screamed at my people's faces.
They planned to tuck me in the obedience pocket.
I had no one in my side so I cupped my hands and knelt down to ask their mercy.
Stop dreaming! They cried out
I yelled in a miserable Tone, my heart sank in fear
They built an ironic box for me but I lived like a bird that sees itself in a larger place although its body is still caged

A brief history of misery

Among the stones, there was a flower that reached out to me.
Many years ago, I dreamt of the Arabian Nights
When I woke up I found myself laughing
Nothing wrong with the laughter
But we shouldn't take history seriously when it turned into a big joke.
I sat at the edge of the battle
Wearing like a warrior
I am not a half person anymore
No Matter how my society categorizes me
No Matter how the world introduces me
I stand in a proud position
Pouring my excitement into the Revolution's womb
I run with all my might seeking a door or a window
I found nothing
I type on my Google page
'Freedom'
I searched many times
But found no results.
I recalled the rooster's sound in our tales
I waited for its appointment
But nothing came.
I shouted like a child
Who had her first sight with gorilla
I moaned
All the women who were hidden under my skin moaned louder.
We are not a family
We are one.
We are tied to each other against the walls of the prison.
It took a very long time to crawl from under the tunnels

Climbing the highest trees
Rubbing our faces with the world's maps
Among the stones, there was a flower that reached out to me.
I was born with a great motivation to scratch the sky
No Matter how many people limited my power
No Matter how hard the world fought me.

The rules of blind obedience

My people hate feeding
The black cats
They say these animals
Are signs of evil
They also refuse
Using salt
They believe
It is a reflection of sadness.
They also treat me
Like a great sin
They imprisoned me in a box
With an opening
For teasing me
From time to time.
I see the light
But couldn't catch it
Next to me a dead fish
Although I am starving
I can't touch it
The fish is powerless
Just like me.
The darkness presses
Against my tongue
My limbs are numb
My wings were lost in a dream.
I am waving to someone
In the mirror
Someone looks like me
In a strange way

Hallucinations

I had a dream of cows lead some people;
Who were humming an old-fashioned poem.
The sound of the flute was coming out from the teeth of an
ancient Oak tree.
In that dream also, there was a moon and a half falling into my
mother's lap
She was stitching a great piece of the sky upon the little heads
of three terrified cats.
I had a dream of being a gorilla
The dirt was caked perfectly with my fingers
I was another version of myself
Peeping into another world
Bathing in another water.
My body had billions of rooms
Empty ones without guests.
I was closed to be a river
But the temptation to be something bigger
Made me kneel
Swerving like a verse
Hovers like an angel's napkin.
Shivers like a love song
In a poet's chest

The age of innocence

When the planet earth swallows all the maps,
The love affection will spread everywhere
I will hang out in your precious land
And you will spend your night
Pacing my room back and forth.
When the maps disappear,
We will replace our fingers with flowers
You will not call me Negro
And I will not laugh at your grandfather's roots.
When the planet earth
Swallows all the maps
We will write our history
By an honest ink
If this happened
People in Madagascar
Will not eat dirt
To escape hunger
When the maps disappear,
I will give you my tongue
To speak my language
And the humanity
Will be the native one
For all of us.

How the war tamed me?

I've been raised by a ghost,
Who used to spin
Around the tombstones
Twice each war.
I am the daughter of
Dust and blood
My eyes swept
The wide streets
Seeking for the light.
We sleep wide-eyed
Covering with the darkness
Shivering from the cold.
The ice between my shoulders
Never melting.
I'm calling my family members
Through my dreams
I see my mother
Walks on her knees
Towards the heaven
In my dreams
She has wings
Like a butterfly.
I've been raised by a nightmare
Which pushed me away
To nowhere
I was surrounded by
The bodies of dead
Holding a ticking bomb
Wondering why am I here
Waiting for going back
To my mother's womb.

Just an invention

Someone planted my body in the heart of your eye
Another one accused you of killing me.
They both said that you had stolen my identity
And buried it deeply in your eye socket.
I was in disbelief my love
Mounting my imagery horse
Counting my sins on my dirty fingers
Humming some old-fashioned poems
Some ancient words that belongs to
An unknown poet
Who had gone with the wind
From a very long age.
When I glance at your eyes
I see mine
Don't fool me
By saying: we are one.
People always tell
You and me similar
In many ways
I considered it a lie
Until the bird which
Pecked at my back
In the wide graveyard
Told me the same.
Someone stitched my existence map
Among the disturbing lines
Which been carved in your Palm.
They attacked you with their papers and TV shows
And no one believes your innocence.
Someone submerged me in your veins
And blamed your despair.

He declared that
You surrounded me by
Pools of salty tears.
I was in disbelief my love
I know this was a rumor
And the truth is
I and you were invented
By that person.

The obedience recipe

I was never told how to draw a sword like a fighter
They just showed me how to zip my mouth like a dangerous
secret lost its way to be revealed.
I was never told how to stand on the top of the world
They just accompanied me to the kitchen for making the
perfect obedience dish
Do you know how many times I had mistaken a Wing for a
chain?
Could you believe that the freedom in my world is considered
a modern stain?
When I was eleven, I tried to free myself from being a caged
girl
First, I ran into our mad streets
I light a million candles around the rusted bodies of the
violence victim's women
When I was young, I stole a half sliver crescent from the sky's
pocket
I was never told how to soar higher
They just took me by the hand before some representatives of
the patriarchal society who have told me what should I do and
what I shouldn't.
They said: don't talk, don't walk, and don't write
You better forget that you have any right

Conspiracy

We sat together on the bridge
Coughing and talking seriously
You introduced yourself as the president of clowns Republic
And I told you that there's much sadness in this truth
And you laughed until your cheeks been swallowed entirely
I saw then your immortal silver teeth
"Don't look at me like that", you said and I did so
Because I have noticed your naked fear
I watched the sky pouring its bluest ink into your eye socket
And I figured out how one could give her a kiss goodbye.
We got too close until my bones touched yours.
I picked up your salt sea tears with my little shaky fingers
The moment you drew a dark circle around my mouth.
"Don't do that", I shouted
And managed to show you my enormous wings
But you turned out into a pair of scissors and aimed to cut
them off.

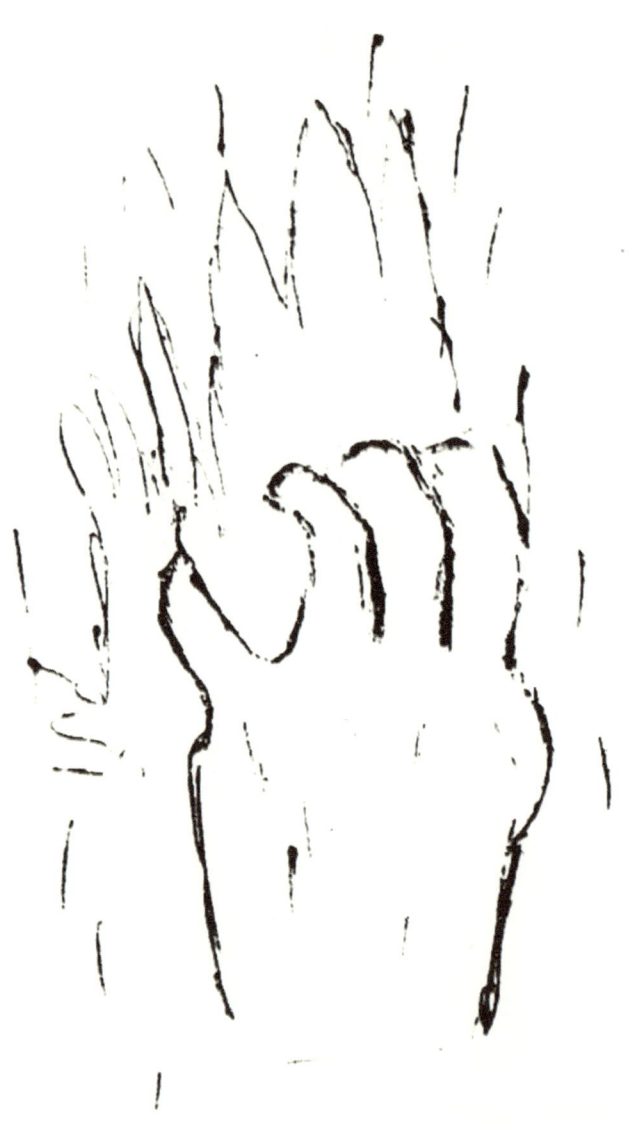

Equality

Somewhere in the world, there is a village that celebrates
justice.
This isn't the Plato ideal city but it is rather the poetic voice
of your heart singing the truth apart from the known clichés,
newsletters terms, and all these differences which separate us
from each other

I want to tell you that at the last time we met
Yes, when you dealt me strangely and considered me a
foreign person to you
I want to announce that before your eyes
It is very easy to admit that we are equals, we are one
But every time we face each other
I encounter my cowardice reflected in you.

The next time I meet you, I will scratch your skin
I promise I will prove that your face is mine
At the edge of your glances, I noticed that recognizable racist
look that warn me to never approach

I know I'm not your family
But I'm your extension and strength
We had the same battle and we have the same goals
And when I contemplate my features in the mirror, I see you
So, please don't categorize me!

After my dad's funeral

After my dad's funeral, I wore his clothes
I still remember how terrible my relatives and neighbors
stared at me.
First, they whispered to each other, then they babbled about
something.
I was my father's daughter and he always taught me that
there's no difference between a man and a woman, but here
in our society, there are many differences between them!
The first time I visited my father's grave, I feel his spirit floating
around me.
It wasn't a kind of horror or Halloween's atmosphere
I really felt that he was trying to kiss me on the cheek.
I read once an interview with a psychic medium who declared
that the dead people see their loved ones and feel them all
the time
Every night I wonder do you see me now.
And what are you doing during this very moment?
Do you eat apples and bananas?
Is there such a thing in your current world?
After your death, I tried to text you many times but they told
me there are no cell phones up there in the other world.

The final scene

During his dying, he planted a group of kisses on the back of my right hand.

I smiled with eyes full of salty tears and kept watching the tiny hidden moon that waved at me from behind his eyelids.

I remember very well how my father used to mix wine and sugar through weaving stories.

I still remember how he used to dip his brilliant poetic words in an ink which made from honey and creativity.

I still hear his breath dancing slow with three little baby Angels and one sunflower crazed by light.

When I was a little girl, my father carried me high on his shoulder while I was humming a funny song and staining his t-shirt with my greasy fingers

He was too busy thinking about how he would nourish his child's character who was born in one of the third world countries.

Confessions of a phenomenal woman

My shoe size is 41, so I have nothing to lose.
I am not your perfect Cinderella!
Your dream girl has a small feet instead I have wings.
"You are my type," you said but like all the free birds, I never ask permission to soar higher.
My maps made of knowledge and freedom.
Could you baby read my newsletters?
You told me once that you are a big fan of the sports magazine, but let me ask could you ever read poetry.
Last night, I spent my hours contemplating your hands lines and found nothing promise.
But you explained that your brightness is stronger than the sun and the lucky lay under your skin.
As a free woman, I danced barefoot on the roof of your mind and you applauded me with a grin.
"Are you strong enough?" You asked
Then, I replied immediately, "why?"
"To be locked up in a golden cage," you answered.
Although, I didn't like your joke at that time, but I smiled back to you from the top of the world years later.

Chasing a ghost

Last night I saw you playing hide and seek with our old fig
tree.
I shouted calling your name with all my might, but you never
heard, just kept swaying gently with your own reflected
shadow on the wall.
Daddy, I'm here still kissing your watery fingers
I'm here still walking around, still looking for your old glasses
to wear instead of mine.
Last night, I saw you dancing on the sand, repeating some
poems and flying from line to line without coming back.
Daddy, I'm here still sitting on your warm couch, still sweeping
all the wide streets seeking for my daddy's body which been
transformed into a butterfly

Violations of women's rights

My teacher made a hole in my forehead,
When I asked him why did you do that?
He laughed and went away.
My uncle loved making jokes about women, one night he
commanded me to sit on the floor and zip my mouth
When I asked him why did you say that?
He laughed and went away.
Our assemblyman doubting the woman's ability
Every session, he makes a victory through hushing a feminine
voice.
When a curious journalist asked him why does he act like
that?
He laughed and went away.
Our sheikh doesn't believe in women's right to work
He also doesn't trust those women who are going out alone
without a male guardian
When his helpless wife asked him
Did our lord require that?
He laughed and went away.
My therapist isn't able to understand my problem,
Every time he repeats
Everything will be okay
Once I asked him
When exactly it will happen?
He laughs and goes away!

Someone I know

Someone I know got rejected three hundred times from the New Yorker but he never gave up.
Although his tears formed a river, he still smile back to each single thing belongs to nature.
He isn't an award winning poet and he never published a book but he could smell the scent of poetry in every corner of life!
Someone I know used to sink his fingers in the deep mud seeking for wisdom.
He hasn't an Instagram page nor a YouTube channel, but he happy with his wheelchair and the smoke of his cheap cigarettes.
Someone I know doesn't get tired of showing his mercy and never stopped feeding a starved dog in the street.
You may notice him in the crowd
A book in his right hand and a flower in the other
Always smile with an open heart able to swallow the whole ugliness of the world and turns it into sugar and wine.

A visit to madhouse

If you planned to visit madhouse,
Don't forget to collect all kinds of flowers for your fellows.
They just like you love flattery and compliment.
If you planned to go there,
Please let ' what you ashamed of' abroad
Because there's much heaviness inside.
And please dress well for not ruin their artistic temperature
Try not to act like a philosopher
Just be an honest human being.
They will respect your frankness and they will surprise you by
applauding and whistling
If you planned to visit madhouse
Don't try to follow the rational people rules.
Just try to laugh and sing your heart out.

A Message to masculine world

No windows in my room, so I could only wrap my body in a
piece of poetry
Showering under the crescent rays.
The world acts like Cinderella's stepmother
Although, I was also lonely but I don't have a witch nor a
charming Prince, so I wonder do I count as a heroine?
Dear world, I still watering your thirsty every dawn
But you bloody monster eat my voice savagely.
Dear world, I don't seek revenge, but you have planted me in
the heart of your crisis and called me a war!
You climbed my high shoulders, grabbed all my apples and
introduced me as a half not a whole person.
You teased me with your silly jokes all over the history
No windows in my room, but there's an identity map in my
chest, so I could breathe in and out through some poetic
letters about the space.

My God and Their Sheikh

At the same time my friend asked me how many people
would enter hell,
I was wondering if there's such a thing!
I love all my friends, Christians, Jew, Buddhist, Even those who
just believe only in Mother Nature.
I know God is merciful enough to love us all without regard to
our individual's religion, cultures and colors.
Every night, God watches over us all, guard us all, sending
kisses and jokes through air to us all.
At the same time my friend laughed at my answers assuring
that our sheikh said the exact opposite and he trust him
because he knows God more than us
I kept smiling and looked higher because I saw God laughing
from behind two silky clouds.

Ode to my father

My father feels better now,
He could move his fingers, able to speak
Now he could stand without a wheelchair and walk without a
walker.
My father feels better now,
He could pointed out at everything everywhere and he could
breathe without coughing or feeling pain
My father feels better now,
Even he could run or fly
Now he could talk without people mistaken what he is saying
Even he could sing without being interrupted.
And who could interrupt the light?
Who in the world could stop the poetic rain from falling and
touching the eager souls?
My father feels better now,
He could swallow easily and now his stricken hands and legs
are good!
Maybe he has wings instead
Maybe he now surrounded by millions balloons made of
poetry
Maybe he is visiting the wisdom kingdom
Maybe he would get from its wisdom some
But the only thing I am certain of is that my father feels better
now because he had gone.

Seeking the light

I was born to a blind mother,
Who used to count the silky stars circled around my neck.
One night, she squeezed until I felt like she was pulling off my skin.
When I tried to shout, I found no voice
My body was cold and silent like a castle
I clapped my hands but she continued her work
I knocked twice on the ground
Nothing happened.
Thirty years ago, mama was a heroine of such a creepy fairy tale
As she told me once, she lost her sight while making a trade with the sun
I laughed at the beginning but later on I cried my eyes out
Day by day, my mother continued to dig until she made a big pool around my neck
I grumble every now and then but mother said this is the best way
To fish out more dreams to lighten our darkness.

Eternal rainbow

The moment you will know where your dead people have gone. You would follow something brighter than religious sermons and self-help books, maybe then, you will be turned into a whole flower or a mystic world. Your silver hair would shift into purple. Your body will be mixed with an eternal rainbow. The moment you will figure out how many holes are carved around your soul, you may stop posting about being the smartest guy on your social media pages. Instead, you will start to learn how to fly without a parachute.

Dancing with an elephant

Imagine there is a black elephant creeping on your jelly belly
while you are taking a nap after a very long day. The elephant
moves his glossy fingers trying to fish out some of your best
memories.
You lay on your dear bed doing your best to keep breathing.
Imagine you try to touch his creamy eyelashes as a way to
steal more songs from his chest. The huge animal agrees to
make an unconditional deal with you.
You cower in a secret corner holding your colorful pen for
drawing your masterpiece. The elephant feels shy. He directs
all his energy into your artwork. Your soul window reveals
more magic.
You play with the animal. Both of you wearing an eternal
smile.
Imagine you decide to dance with your black elephant
throwing jokes through his giant ears. The more you succeed
in making him laugh, the more pleasure he gives.
Each of you climbs the highest candy mountain, you love the
feeling.
You long badly to repeat the experience. You behave
automatically without wondering what if the elephant got
angry in the midst of the game?!

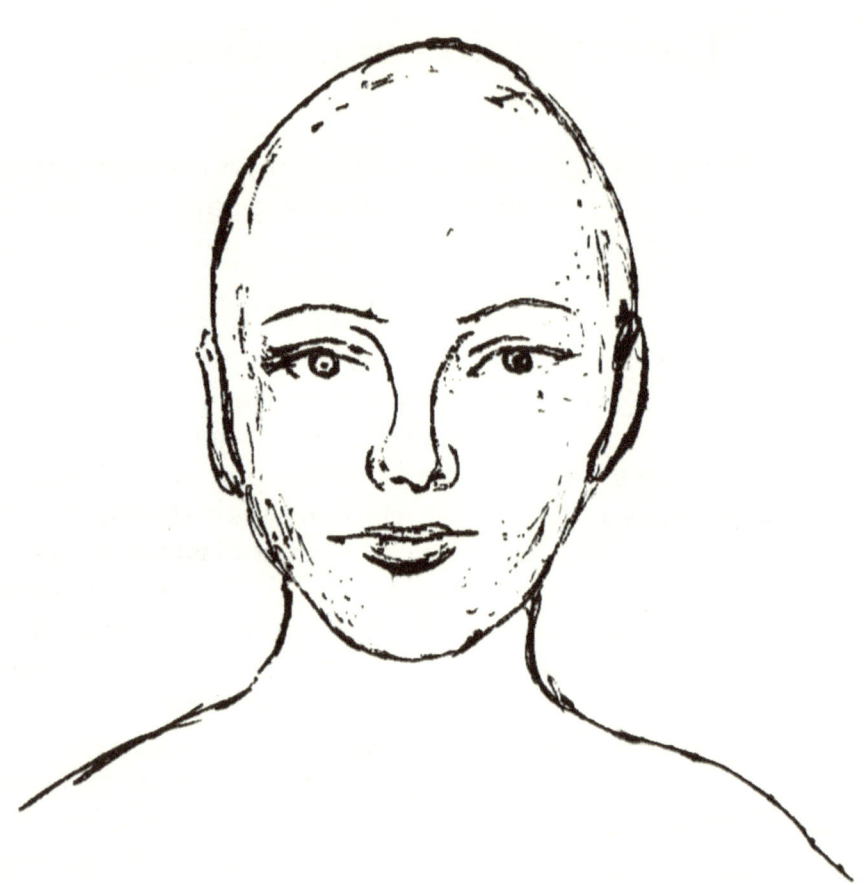

Strange case of a bald woman

Being born bald is a dangerous matter which requires much security. Imagine that you raise a hairless kid. Such a terrible feeling, right? That's what my mother felt.

Imagine your head is nothing but a naked ball while you live in a world where everybody wears feathers, leather, and golden wigs.

Ashamed of my baldness, creeping toward the ground holes like a rabbit.

I was seeking to hide in a secret place between some person's thighs or deeply in the cave of an eye.

The story began when the authorities decided to cut off the umbilical cord of the pregnant women themselves to make sure there is no mother carrying a dreamful child.

I still remember how I slept wide-eyed in my mother's womb.

My body quivered like a candy-shaped wish. I was dreaming of swallowing the delicious sky and going far away with my limitless ideas.

The officials stopped in their positions feeling trapped. This happens every time they found a newborn child shaking hands with colorful imagination.

Nothing scarier than having a third eye, they thought raising their weapons toward us.

My mother fell on her knees &the moment her salty tears settled on my little head didn't leave me.

Vision

Mother told me that my great-grandfather was a human being. I asked her what the exact definition of such a weird term is. She answered after short laughter it means nothing but a silly joke. She used to water my thirst with these funny tales while shaking her silky tail every now and then.

I climbed her shoulders with great motivation to reach the highest spot as usual. My mother raised her fork-shaped hand swaying like thunder humming some old songs.

One hundred light years before, we circled around each other listening to our leader's speech. He was talking about the last human being who lived on the earth. That man who thought himself very smart and attractive.

"He was lonely and scared." our leader shouted in the space adding that though the poor creature never stopped trying, he lost himself at the end of the story.

We stand in awe, we had no idea that there were any other creatures except us.

I longed to meet my grandfather, my desire grew more urgent when I knew that the creature who fell in love with my grandmother was calling her "my beloved alien!"

Imagine that there was a creature who has two eyes, one mouth, and a brilliant imagination!

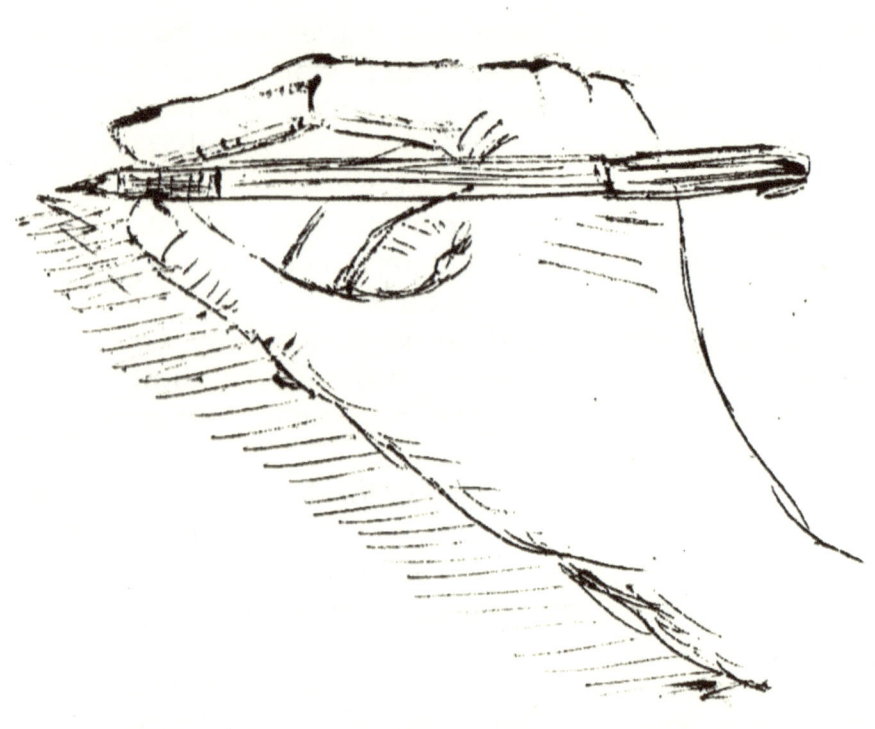

Poetry

I'm scared, so I write poetry
I suppose you are scared too because you read poetry.
Each of us decided to dig a hole in the ground to reach out to
the other hand of our fate.
Do you see my reflection in your own mirror?
Are you too tied to some winged soul?
The mint tastes salty down here in my depth. My biological
clock moves backward. I hear you shout:
me too. Don't put your right hand on your heart o swear.
There is nothing scarier than doing that. I'm in your shoes, my
friend. Touch my skin with your finger.
Do you feel my coldness? I'm freezing out there shivering like
a daydream. Don't let my hand fall down.
My heart is crowded with music and whiffs. Introduce me to
your ego & tell me does he feel satisfied?
I'm scared my love, every single letter quivers on the paper
like a frightened little cat confronting ice rainfall.
I'm very scared, so let us share poetry.

Rumor about the sun

The sun disappeared. We have all heard the rumor millions of
times. Somebody stole the star replacing it with a fake emoji.
We tired from looking here and there. We ran to the streets
seeking the invisible light but nothing was found. I myself
searched thousand times in my coat pocket. Nothing. Nothing
at all. How dare someone do such a thing? Who is he? We
can't raise our eyes. We couldn't bear our burdens.
We wear many faces except the true one, but the sun? What
about the sun?
People move blindly, time travels with no return (there is
no time machine here) & mama still cooking her porridge
as a humble way to fight hunger. Everybody asks: don't
you see the sun? Our darkness lasts, our duties are never
accomplished & we sing without music.
At the beginning, we said that its disappearance never stop
us, but lately, we changed our minds &gone to the tops of our
trees.

Random talk

Every time I plan to read a self-help book. I change my mind.
What is the hell the author is going to tell? Let it go? Focus on
the positive energy? Don't forget to meditate? I ask myself.
Every time such an idea flashes in my mind I leave her as
soon as possible & going to our roof to figure out how many
neighbors are staring at our dirty curtains. Did god create
the world in six days? I think trying to collect myself & the
Breadcrumbs together.
The village children playing hide and seek with their hunger.
My old uncle still winking to a pretty girl & my mother stitches
the last piece of her patience.
I feel jealous of all those who believe in self-help books.
Those who know very well how to take a selfie with the
luxurious mirror behind them. Those who couldn't skip a little
moment without sharing.
People who post about their achieved bucket list year after
year. those who long to buy one of Picasso's artwork not
because they love Pablo Picasso but because they want to be
called "art collectors"
I feel jealous of those who don't have the ability to distinguish
between literature and beauty magazines but insist to write
critical reviews. Every time I decided to read a self-help book,
I look at my cocktail bird feeling that he is laughing at me.
i want badly to be like that one who says life is a piece of cake.
I desire to go to many places just for taking pictures not to
have fun

Kindness

If you want to know something, don't Google it. Just search deeply within you. Last night, I thought of the kindness meaning. I tapped on the keyboard. The dictionary definition appeared on the screen. Nothing else. I know that meaning, so I chose to see more images related to the searched word. I found many stretched-handed poor boys sitting in the dirt under someone's mercy. Some cute girls looked miserable waiting for your financial support. African single mothers breaking the rocks under the heat.

Indian children wanted to be fed up. Egyptian beggars wandering the wide streets. A European blind man wants somebody to take care of him. Some American orphanage house needs volunteers. Some Arabic old paralyzed woman seeks healthy aid & finally, a group of Asian children holding empty pots stare at the camera.

I closed the pages. That wasn't what I'm looking for.

I wanted more than this. I tried to pronounce the word softly between me and myself. I repeat what I did many times.

My heart moved slowly. I decided to add more rhythm and delight. The word "kindness" danced on the edges of my tongue.

I felt warmth surrounding my libs. A poetic voice clutched the core of me. I swayed like a feather trying my best to count my sighs.

The carnation grew between my fingers. I believed that my body was lighter than the dream. Billions of rooms showed themselves inside.

The dream-eater

I was dreaming of hearing some voice scratching the heart
of my ear. Standing half-naked on my tippy-toes crawling
toward a cell peopled by rats and desires. Don't. I said to the
dream-eater, that one who gets ready every night to eat my
sweetness with knife and fork.

Every day I wake up forgetting what my dream was? I'm not
Alzheimer's patient but I feel like I live in two different worlds.
Is that a particular disease? I don't think so, it is a delicious
kind of suffering. My father passed away the last year. He was
laughing then he died. Everything around me became dark
and gloomy. Everything even the bright sky. I swear I thought
of contacting a physic medium. I didn't want to know where
did he hide his money pocket or his preferred glasses frame.
I just desired to know how he feels right now. Does his soul
indulge in a pool of honey? Had he gone to a darkened cave?
I was afraid that he would go to hell because he lied once
when he told me he will never ever leave me.

The letter

Writing a formal letter isn't a piece of cake, especially when you sitting down bare feet. The shoes are very important. They are the best, but what could a man do if he hasn't any? Although there is no absolute in the whole world, I believe shoe matter.

Thirty years I inherited my father's shoes but they are gone now. Don't think I'm a beggar, I'm a gentleman who used to be beaten and insulted all day by his beloved wife.

Only last night I decided to rebel. My wife respected that however, she couldn't accept it. I shouted. This is the first time I express my anger. She raised her eyebrow wondering what is next. I tapped the ground with my wrinkled feet. She sighed. I tired. We sat beside each other exhausted. I felt weak again &told her that I wrote a former letter to the king for getting a new pair of shoes. She gasped then cried. It was the first time to see her tears.

The next day the authorities took away her shoes and we both became bare feet.

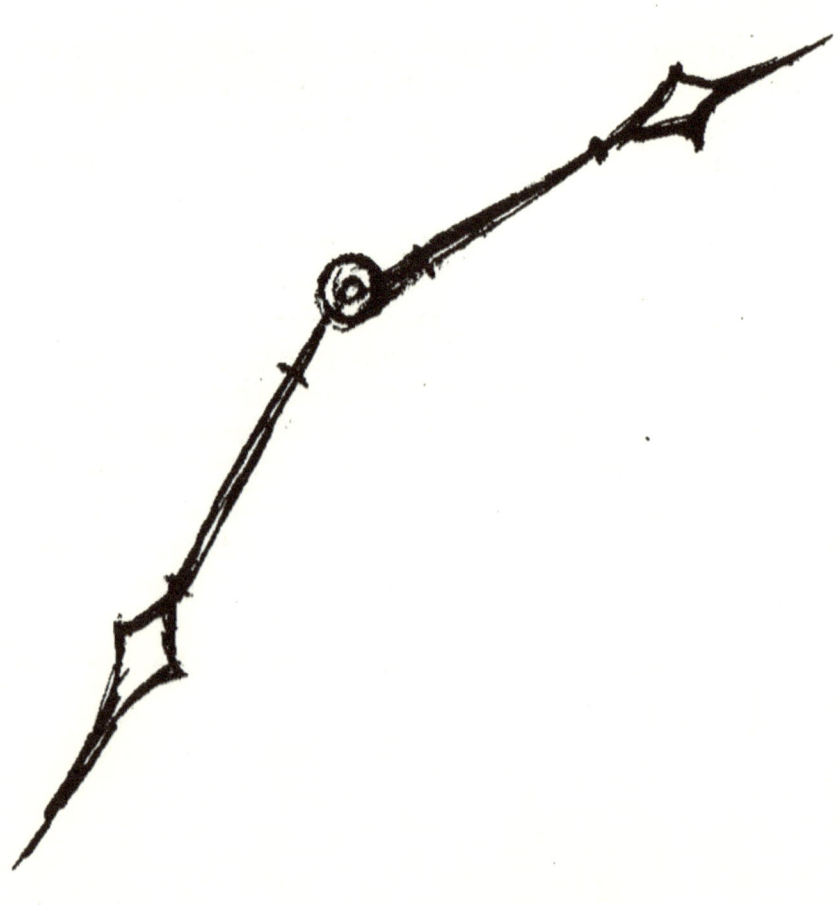

The Art of Living a Lie

Time is our own invention. No need to calculate hours, seconds, days, and years. God didn't create the calendar. He just put an endless sky giving us hopes to reach it. We crowded in each corner stretching our hands like beggars. The sun was too close. She kept watching. The moon waved and laughed. The other universes played hide and seek. We run into the wide forest seeking wings and light. We found language. We didn't know how it works? Moving our tongues and lips in a helpless way. Nothing came out. We tried pressing on and on. Nothing came out. Not a word.
We squeezed the upper bottom of our souls. Nothing happened. After billions of years, we decided to call things by its name. If we feel hungry, we say it is lunchtime. If lust knocks on our inner door, we say let's have sex.
If we feel lonely, we announce an urgent working meeting.
If we feel scared we write books and make movies. If we feel bored, we invent other public holidays.
Our fellow animals grew smaller. We entered them into cages and prisons. No cell is big enough to endure our grief. God didn't create clocks and stopwatches, we just invent a brilliant way to smooth ourselves slowly.

Does the moon kneels?

I got married to the moon. Not the bloody version, I'm not
a Halloween fan but that crystal full one. Our first contact
began only with a rope. While sharing somebody's dream, he
looked at me, I stretched my hand for reaching out. He sent
a universal kiss. I wore a sliver smile. He took my light hand
away hanging it around a fairy's neck.
Butterflies walked on my naked body. I hide my secret
between his eyes. He murmured saying "I love you" in another
poetic language. Me too, I said without knowing how to date
the moon?
One night he decided to sing. I was listing while eating
grapes like that the first for me &the second for him. He also
whispered wrapping the whole starry night around my waist.
He tried to amuse me in many different ways. I loved all his
games except hide and seek.
One night, I thought of hugging him. I threw a very long rope
but he didn't appear. Until now I still wonder does the moon
kneels.

The dance of life

While you are sleeping in your mama's womb you have a
creepy vision. Two buffalos dragging your body towards a
cameraman. You move your fatty belly from right to lift as a
stupid way to prove that you are not hungry anymore. Some
mysterious smell flatter in the air like an unfinished task. You
start to cry & laugh at the same time.
The two animals indulged their pointed fingers in a pool of
dirt. They painted your whole face while dancing on their
tippy-toes. The scene lacks Surrealism. You know certain
words from an ancient age. You try to shape them into your
lips. God watching you as usual. He waves in amusement.
Numerous trees grow between your thighs. You crawl toward
single laughter escaping from an angel's chest. You see the
world with an open eye.
A woman sitting under you playing with the time machine.
She makes a fuss but no one punishes her. You contemplate
the world in awe. You love to whisper even when you don't
know what to say.
The two buffalo returned again lifting your body to the level
of the Seventh Heaven.
You watch million flying fish nursing their babies. A man looks
at you. He wears some messy clouds. You think it is not real.
You say it is just my imagination.
A group of poets embracing mint leaves. Crystal water circles
their brownish necks. They bite a bread-shaped poem. You
feel amazed. Who am I? You ask. Where am I? You repeat.
God still watching. He composes a fresh play. You want to take
a look. He knows that. Some of his precious papers fall down
intently until reaching your feet. You read it. You feel a sudden
shiver. Everything turns upside down. You close your eyes
again & keep moving inside your mother's kingdom.

How to start a conversation

Don't ask a woman how old is she. Don't ask a man too. We all hide our identity papers carefully wanting no one to peek. I still remember the last time I told it. I was twenty-five. Such a perfect age. It suits everything love, ambition, marriage, travel, and parachuting.

My never married aunt lives in a cave. She entered the place after reaching thirty. Now she is sixty. The misery began when a driver's car asked her how old she is.

Our neighbor struggling with aging. He was tired from counting his days

every now and then he penetrates his wife's eyes trying to figure out where his years have gone?

Our garden flowers turn into swarming snakes at the moment somebody asks how old we are. It is a scary question. Don't ask anybody how old is he because the literal translation here is how long do you feel a stranger on earth?

Prayers

The terrified little kitten that I saw trembling under the oak
was praying.
Her soft whisper stole my attention.
It made me notice how many times the brunch waves to the
sky& how quick the latter kneels to pick up one billion kisses
in the second.
The last drop of water that touched my sweaty palm was
praying.
I can feel its music flowing between my fingers.
I am sitting down face to face with my injuries
I keep silent while watching a butterfly making a grand piece
of poetry
the great art she makes
the small pain I feel
listen. How holy prayers she recites
listen, how poetic voices that I hear.

Healing process

God knows more than this.
This is the usual universal game.
we all play hide and seek with ourselves
thinking that we will find something worthy
you still laugh at your face in front of the mirror
and the former still asking more eternal questions
you lost your mind many years during your mysterious
existence in the womb.
Exactly like you,
I still boil the water while wondering
why on earth I am here.
my own doctor suggests
telling funny stories
instead of taking pills
he is sure that laughter matters
last night, I tried to please him
I started hugging the trees, swallowing a whole star
and things became better.

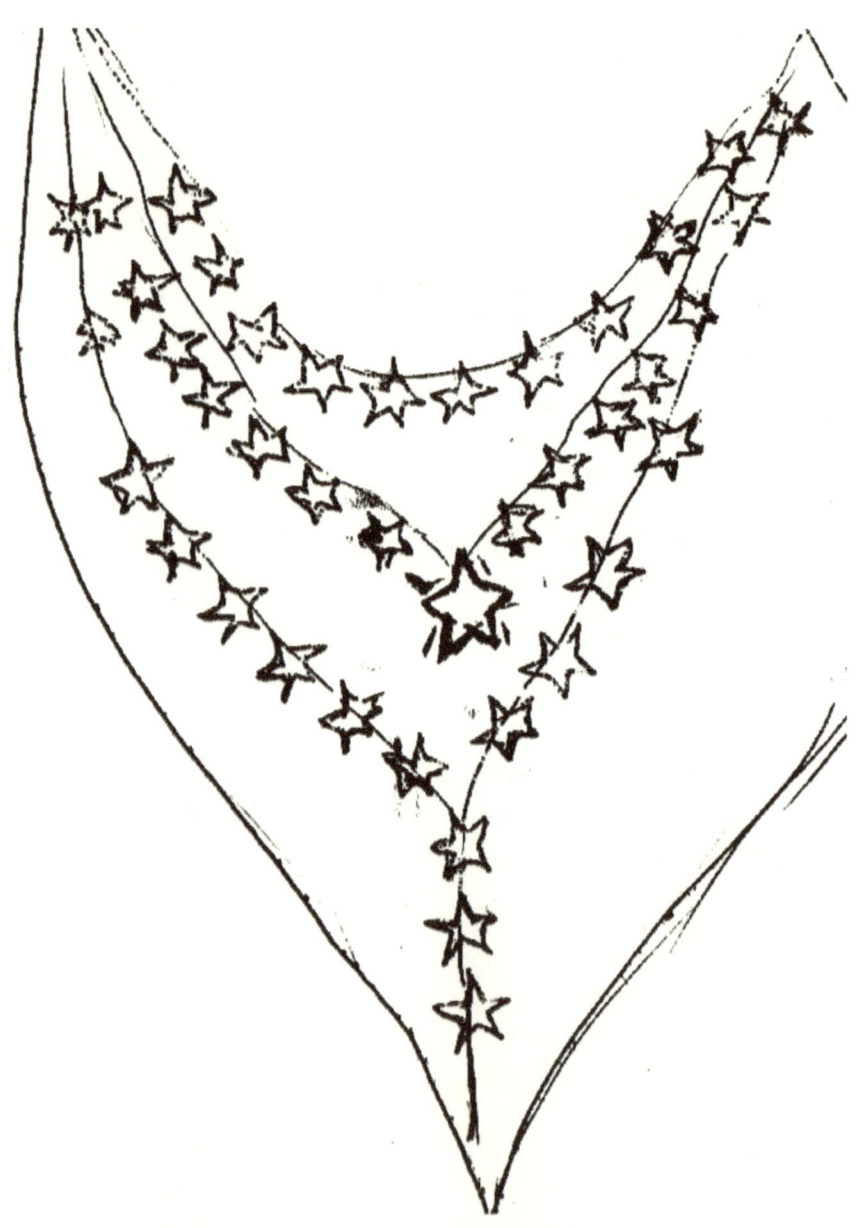

Miracles

I believe in miracles,
That delicious kind of magic
Like traveling through balloons of poetry
Or seeing an angel pouring a glass of joy for needy children.
I believe in miracles,
When someone bakes a loaf of bread for a stranger.
That kind of pure love
When a group of different people fish out the bright stars
circled around the waist of Justice Galaxy
I believe in miracles,
Counting all the mint leaves that grew between my fingers as
a poetic leader to the sky.
I believe in miracles,
Sending a universal kiss to an orphan girl living in another
country talking another language.
I believe in miracles
That precious kind of peace that makes your heart sing.

Injustice

Injustice tastes like swallowing your own salty tears,
It's like smothering your only pet who always loves you.
You are lonely in the darkness crawling on your naked belly
You are incapable of eating your worries before they grow
and eat you.
Injustice sharp as a knife
It's that kind of complicated feeling which you can't translate
on Google.
Watch it from afar, you will find a creepy bogyman put out his
tongue at you. Don't take one step closer, you will fall into the
trap.

Transformation

I dream of cockatoo birds sipping milk from the sky
I fly from corner to corner holding sugar, wine, and more
funny jokes.
God is up sitting on his throne watching how the earth dances
under my bare feet.
Kisses, wishes and more than that riding silver horses.
Creamy cloud falling down close to my head singing an old
song.
My bones covered by the rhythm. My tongue turned into
a butterfly. I sway in the air thinking of the worlds I pass
dreaming of more honey rivers to have more fun, wondering
how many orphan girls still live within me.
I try to raise both hands throwing them to a new universal
castle. I feel new again. I sense more than being alive. There is
something beyond happiness. There is delicious beyond joy.
Believe me, there is music you have never heard of.

Confessions of a ghost

I used to dream big,
Not the kind of dreams you learned in school and the university.
As a full-time funny ghost,
I used to love my job earnestly.
You may find me in the abandoned cirques, playing hide and seek with many other wandering spirits or you may see me playing video games with fresh corpses under the ground.
Believe me, technology is not just for living people.
I too have the same right to play.
Trust me, ghosts have a great sense of humor.
We shake each other hands. Wave when we were far away.
Use Google many times and guess what?
We make funny memes.
The only difference is that our world is free from lies and taxes.

Daily struggle

How many times did you lose yourself?
My therapist asks,
I sit on the couch preparing myself to count on my fingers.
One hundred times, I say
One thousand? He asks
One million, I say
One billion? He asks
I laugh.
My therapist laughs too.
We both know that the numbers are a very funny thing to tell.
I think of people who wronged me,
People who cheated on me.
I remember how their grayish faces looked after playing the
victim role each time we faced.
My therapist looks deeply into my eyes.
It happens again.
A huge swirl of salty tears
Circled around.
As usual,
He tries his best to rescue me from drowning.

Meeting a fig tree

I know a fig tree walks in beauty singing a fair song as soon as
my heart beats.
She uses elevators& electric stairs
People are astonished by her actions, but she doesn't even
bother to argue with them.
She is very busy with counting the blessings on her enormous
fingers.
I see a wild bird waving at everybody,
Running in hurry to different errands.
She understands what poetry means through silence.
Sometimes I feel as if I am a pond& millions ducks swimming
around my waist
A crystal ball comes from somewhere at my feet,
My world turns upside down when I touch it
I locked in a fountain of light,
Here I am sitting peacefully with many versions of me.

In the cell

You wake up early as usual,
Looking at your broken mirror,
You try to imitate the clown's features for the fifth time.
You couldn't laugh anymore
Because you aren't the same person you were yesterday.
People change.
You stand moving your tired legs,
Thinking of all those friends, family members& neighbors you
lost so far.
You are all alone in your painted room,
Keeping building castles from memories.
You are afraid of losing your mind but the idea excited you,
Forcing you to listen to your old audio records while giving a
glimpse at your old photos.
In the photos, you seem idiot& fat with a happy smile.
You look better now,
You seem clever
You have muscles.
Perhaps it is time now to regain your smile.

Amirah Al Wassif is a freelance writer based in Egypt. Her prolific output includes general interest articles, novels, short stories, songs, and of course, poetry. Five of her books have been written in Arabic and much of her English work has appeared in a great many cultural magazines. Her work has been translated into Spanish, Kurdish, Hindi and Arabic.

Amirah Al Wassif's poems have appeared in several print and online publications including *South Florida Poetry, Birmingham Arts Journal, Hawaii Review, The Meniscus, The Chiron Review, The Hunger, Writers Resist, Right Now*, and others. Amirah also has a poetry collection, *For Those Who Don't Know Chocolate* (Poetic Justice Books & Arts, 2019) and *How to Bury a Curious Girl,* and a children's book, *The Cocoa Boy and Other Stories* published in February 2020.